SCIENTIFIC MARVEL

SCIENTIFIC MARVEL

Poems

CHIMWEMWE UNDI

ANANSI

Published in Canada in 2024 and the USA in 2024 by House of Anansi Press Inc. houseofanansi.com

28 27 26 25 24   1 2 3 4 5

Library and Archives Canada Cataloguing in Publication

Title: Scientific marvel : poems / Chimwemwe Undi.
Names: Undi, Chimwemwe, author.
Description: Includes bibliographical references.
Identifiers: Canadiana (print) 20230547559 | Canadiana (ebook) 20230547567 | ISBN 9781487012250 (softcover) | ISBN 9781487012281 (EPUB)
Subjects: LCGFT: Poetry.
Classification: LCC PS8641.N35 S35 2024 | DDC C811/.6—DC23

Cover design: Greg Tabor
Cover image: Adapted from an image by Creative Photo Focus/iStock Images
Book design and typesetting: Ellie Hastings

House of Anansi Press is grateful for the privilege to work on and create from the Traditional Territory of many Nations, including the Anishinabeg, the Wendat, and the Haudenosaunee, as well as the Treaty Lands of the Mississaugas of the Credit.

Canada Council   Conseil des Arts
for the Arts   du Canada

ONTARIO ARTS COUNCIL
CONSEIL DES ARTS DE L'ONTARIO
an Ontario government agency
un organisme du gouvernement de l'Ontario

With the participation of the Government of Canada
Avec la participation du gouvernement du Canada | Canadä

We acknowledge for their financial support of our publishing program the Canada Council for the Arts, the Ontario Arts Council, and the Government of Canada.

Printed and bound in Canada

CONTENTS

SCIENTIFIC MARVEL

PROPERTY 101

This I know how to do: reduce a person to their facts
unsympathetic to condition, either useful
or distinct. Good practice is dissolving my beloved
into traits, serving the language that I serve, and work against,
to dupe. I am advised that an example of violence
is not violence, like a photograph in a museum,
transformed by the lens and then by display. Because I am
advised I turn advisory, surmise the gaps were not
openings through which to shine my particular night,
dark as the din of this country's measured silence.
This is to say I am learning about property
in a recent nation where no one looks me in the eye.
What spectacle elides by calling itself analysis:
hallways, riddled with exits, each an error to pass.

WINNIPEG POEM

1. A reference to the famously frigid winters, often by way of reference to winter clothing or activities

2. For obvious reasons, the phrase "prairie sky"

3. Lamenting (general)

4. Lamenting (winter-specific)

5. Invoking John K. Samson, explicitly or by prosody

6. A reference to the history of the name *Winnipeg*, being "murky water" in Inínímowin

7. A passing or rote reference to Indigenous peoples, broadly (post ~2015, apologetic in tone)

8. A mention of local flora, typically in metaphor (e.g., lilac, chokecherry, birch, milkweed, Saskatoon berry, thistle, goldenrod, prairie grass, etc.)

9. A mention of local fauna, typically in metaphor (e.g., deer tick, blackfly, skeeter, cankerworm, pigeon, crow, etc.)

10. A reference to the forking of the Red and Assiniboine Rivers, and/or to the Forks

11. A reference to Salisbury House ("Sals"), and pre-2019, Stella's restaurants

12. Portage & Main and/or Confusion Corner and/or the Golden Boy

13. Invoking Guy Maddin's *My Winnipeg*, explicitly or in tone

14. Grain, etc.

ESCAPOLOGY
after Dean Gunnarson

The opposite of a boat
is a pine vessel

built to hold a body
keen to sink.

The river is named
for the same russet silt

Grandma Ruby would tuck
two-fingered

into inside her cheek,
suck dry like marrow

from a bone, saliva pooling
under tongue. I'd bet it tastes

like clanging sounds,
like blood does, like cuffs

lick bruises into wrists.
Is it still magic

if I built the cage? Ask the
crowds cantillating.

I wanted something
too, to survive,

besides my good name.
And I was not hungry

when they pulled me
from the banks.

I was dead.
I was blue, and fed

a medic's air. I was filled
to the brim with the river,

and what reds it, and myself.
Tell me: How is that not magic?

Because I chose that water?
Because I chose those chains?

TO POINT IF POSSESSED
from *R v Grant*, 2009 scc 32

[176] ███here ███ of course, ████████████████████████
████████ the ████████████████████████
██
████████████████████ hypothetical ████████ 'reasonable person' ████
██
████████████████████████ As mentioned, ████████ is
black. ████████████████████████████ is ████████████ free
████████ to walk ████████████████ to███ wish████
██
████████████████████████ to ████████████████████
██
████████████████████████ point████████████████
████████████ if ████████████ possessed ████████████████
████████ to shed light on ████████ liberty ████████████████
████████████

GRUNTHAL, MANITOBA (2019)

A beautiful country, so full of breath
The sky as wide open as a howling throat

      My throat as wide open as a prairie sky
      As blue, as hungry to ungive what's been taken

You can't give back what has been taken
Unname the place named what it already is

      Rename a place that was already named
      In language with altitude and implication

This language's altitude and implication
Good for making art and telling lies

      Good for making art on telling lies
      For making promises it meant to keep

Made promises we had no means to keep
Renamed the place already named

      Renamed the place already named
      Sixty-four clicks northeast of nothing

Sixty-four clicks northeast of nothing
Ninety-five clicks south of nothing

      Fifteen miles southwest of nothing
      A beautiful country because you still breathe

MY COUNTRY

In common with my country
a disinterest in survival
a vague belief in a god that fails
to guide my actions
except when it suits me
two too-big hands at the end
of hanging arms and a way
with prepositions, witnessing
desperation in effects
instead of causes. I mean
my country the way
my country means
my country
and what else is there to say?
I am bad and brown
and trying. Nothing here
belongs to me or
could or ever will.

SALT

Who the scholars name
in fractions. In whose mirror
my mouth rives, longing
my vowels.

In whose before, whose after.
Whose split, wet and roiling self,
head and hand misread
greeting from shore.

Whose life a woman screened
in two, the second in big jeans.
What other nation is not in me.
Who is sick for homes

called home in lies.
Who thanks ancestors
for this fine life but can't
pronounce their names.

SONG FOR ENDLING, UNBORN

We have jam jars, from Christmas,
so we start there. My eggs

and his eyes, viscid on the yellow
sill, floating like sliced peaches

in real juice. In the bathroom,
where the light is best,

with the door closed
so the cat can't lap liquid

from the mouth,
left open to aerate and stir gently,

like the book says to do.
In the dark, I scold myself

for being too afraid
and not afraid enough.

Think, better this
than three-fourths of one

year making a promise
that is also a betrayal.

We can barely promise now,
never mind a future

to suffer through.
We'll raise you,

pin our hopes to you,
explain what birds were,

and waterfalls, how
you started on a windowsill,

then a countertop Tupperware
where you rose to flesh like yeast,

fed the spiked thing inside me
that turns me all edges. It's hard

to explain, so I won't.
Like all daughters of your year,

you will hear me crying
from the hallway,

see me emerge chipper
and lacking explanation,

twisting open yellow cans of beans.
He will awake with your soft

hair in his mouth.
Watching you churn

in your thrifted glass, I hope
you beat this ending here,

and no one mistakes you for a left thing
and feeds your dark liquid

to the thirst in their mouth.

SUBPLOT

local disaster / I writhe through / at the clinic / I am
careful / to need the pills / without asking / to explain
/ they do not / pass / seamlessly / from respite / to
chemical respite / the agony / when baton / hits ground
/ beside me / how embarrassing / to need / and selfish
/ small print / still / filled with the big / kith and kin
and colour / postal code / the very gist of me / the
doctor's sigh / an echo / his neck stretch / a reflex / he
recommends / I get more sleep / the big / funnelled /
through wound / in me / my blood / historied / but
in me / emptying me / and me / alone / writhing / on
shrinking side / in shrinking light

BLACK AT THE TIME
from *R v Grant*, 2009 scc 32

[154] A ████ body ████████████

████████████████ at ████ risk ████████████

████████ their ████████████████████

████████████████████████ Arbitrary ████████

Function████████████████████████████

████████████ The ████████████ Conception of ████

████████████████████████████████

████████████████ *Cost* ████████████████

████████████████████████████████

████████████ black████████████████

████████

[155] At the ████ time,████████████████

██ approached and asked questions████████████

██ unable to choose ████████████████ and ████

████████ possess ████████████████████

████████████████████████ perspective ██ the

encounter is not made known by words ████████

ON THE IMMINENT DESTRUCTION OF PORTAGE PLACE MALL

not a bomb   but levelled   still   unkeeling
listless or lacking inventory   shortly, nothing

shortly, unmade   hearkening back to blondes
on VHS   stockings named   for favoured subset of flesh
glitter rides the escalator's churn

jingle dirges in the backlight   spectre
backlight blue   geometrical   impossible
this edifice: "the biggest thing to hit the city

since the flood"   flood displaced in meaning
by a bigger flood   mall displaced
in meaning by the flood of us

flood again   toxic metaphor
begat by bordering   Black and brownness
by bodies   blued   bluing   made buoyant
by the mass of us   liquid in our number

to be sure   us ≠ this keen city   nostalgic amnesiac
supplicant lustrated in silted water   ten tented fingers
breaks for wagging

us ≈ my people   connotes a buoyant mass   joyous noise
gestures to uncle strangers
in the food court   stuffing ears with courage   lies

in Dollarama   auntie compliments my accent
offers me her son   strained plaid polyester
Portage Place First Nation   which D says
to mean ≈   my people

people made a demographic   disappeared
from municipal imagination   struck like noon
inside exit doors locked into exterior walls

before unmaking   again return to the blueness
of the light   gossamer and permanent   to the trees
indoors at that   a rube's early wonder

to these planters built for sitting   uniformed men
imported from the suburbs to tell us not to sit

to the clock's bright mechanics   spiral
torsions only visible coming down the escalator
blunt blade also promised better things

the trouble is how to build it   the blue unmade
amidst mist and wind and unhurried anarchy
how to conjure house and universe

even dexterous in this new split tongue
I am full of all the wrong language   full of little
but language   lungs full of elsewhere's smoke

I am helpless   before what can't be helped   mouth busied
retuning the questions: what beautiful thing
has ever left me and returned?

what else in the middle distance is burning?

WHAT BIRDS WERE

Yes, animals, and small, and spined –
      no, not unlike a dog,
            say *dog*, but with feathers.

And not always, and not always small.
      Oh, a feather is a kind of
            leaf. They were good, the birds, yes,

and some of them were kind of bad.
      They made eggs – you've seen an egg,
            remember? Oh, flight is a kind of movement

that acknowledges its limitations.
      A beak is like a sharp mouth. This same sky,
            say *sky*, but blue, and before falling –

and you would look and there would be –
      yeah, small animal, that's close,
            with a body of bones so light it grew wings,

            say *wings*, instead of hands.

GIRLS WHO
after Joelle Barron

Girls doubled up in the stall, smoke tickling
over the peeling door. Spray the air with
Britney Spears Circus Fantasy
after second bell,
reluctant retreat to classroom.

Girls who pull the denim up around your flesh,
hands cold against your dark belly,
who envy the big and small of you,
fill up on ginger ale, cotton wool in orange juice,
a trick she read online. Backward tilting,
good hair in high and holy ponytail,
yellowing arc of teeth bound in braces
in a way that makes you want braces.

Girls with small hands,
and big brothers,
and riding boots,
who know what a mickey is,
and where to get one.
Who would look back,
become a willing pillar.

Girls who have soccer after, or dance.
Girls who looked away
and uninvited us from sleepovers.
Easy retractors of the ST END half-heart,
smirk less apologetic than glad not to be sorry.
Eyes wide under purple
shadow, henna butterflies
on the small of their wrists.

Girls in group chats or drunk in bathrooms,
handing out tuck tape, tampons
and hair ties, slurred compliments
that send you spinning out into the night.

Girls watched by everyone,
who join in, make mirrors of everything,
and me, quick study, slow to speak,
slow to notice when they're watching back.

Girls with mouths as sticky as the dance floor,
as hard to pull away from. Girls with heart emojis
next to your name who avoid you in the hallway.
Girls with new boyfriends,
and bigger plans,
and questions you're the answer to,
who move to the suburbs,
get a pug,
lose your number,
grow out their bangs.

360 PORTAGE

A city is a series of decisions. All that distance,
built. Here, the glass glints, vague as water,

sentinel of the some, sustained. My proximity
will collapse in the old ways: join the dogs
wilding the edge of each field.

Trees interrupt the cement, roots muffled
and implied. I could not name them

or, sure, my neighbours. A long exposé
on a short walk from here. I want to take the blame,
being so used to taking. The story of the story

I have liked being told. What happened while I kept
my eyes where directed. When I left it

to the architects to scrape the shrinking sky.
Elsewhere, a fish is split like two lips,
spits pine needles and fails its way up a ladder.

A clean, green engineering marvel. A card
in one memory up some other sleeve. A growing

hunger for power in the South is fed.
Some hands are configured to wring,
to pull blood, to plunder. Other names lose

their meaning. First the sleight, then an unveiling.
I take my stories before bed.

Questions like milk teeth, deciduous
and doomed. Efficiency, too, is formed

in the mouth, sharp
and reddest at the root.

GOOD MOMS

are beige
floral
fibreglass measured
in months do not have
their father's
hands do not
read the news
have eyes
on the back
of their heads
are wide
paths pink
with shadow
say
I'm sorry
and by that
mean sorry
say *I can tell*
you are having big
feelings
right now
are warm
as a winter
coming
have neither
a history nor good
troubled skin are
therapized
crystallized
fine static
bright behind the eyes
let you come
inside them
and let it
change
their name

BLOTTER

Two in the food court, thumbs tucked by baton.

Two on my way to the gym, one smiling at a little kid.

Three in blue, brand new, biking down Graham.

Four in a row, making room on the sidewalk, red cups in hand.

One type at the bus stop, checking handfuls of change.

A dozen hundred after dinner, damned.

By the river, that time, by speedboat, three on bikes, some in cars, we didn't count, some on foot, in bulletproof vests, collaring some guy.

By the bus shelter, crushing cardboard.

One type in the skywalk, urging people to their feet.

Two at our neighbours, chasing, asking questions.

One type in my body, in my index finger's bones.

In the news, like a hand is in a sock.

In a Terradyne Gurkha MVP.

Six, between Langside and Furby, one ponytail swishing and a knee in someone's side.

Six, later, between us, futile with regret.

In a rotor whirring, tail boom overhead.

Like a bird and instead of birds and thus, and otherwise, sounding in my sleep, filling, I think, what distance has ruptured.

In the air, again, that frequent wail.

At Superstore, by those chocolate bars up front, thumbs tucked by baton.

In the budget, by an arrow, green and pointed at the sky.

A BLACK WALK
from *R v Grant*, 2009 SCC 32

[5]　　a　black　walk

the　past

testified　an unusual　and continued

time

a　purpose for being

seen　maybe　a

want　a

were　to monitor

anyway　in

light　or　plainclothes

or concern.

TAYLER IM AT 412 FURBY LEE
ekphrasis for graffiti at Young & Broadway

& what is aerosol's lineage if not a beckoning. & what is worth spraying if it isn't an oath. I mean, worse things have yellowed this corner, & folded it to something to pass between palms. & maybe any map is a better god than this brick. & if architecture speaks, who gets to spell out what it says. & yes, the flowers are fading out of hue. & yes, you can see it from every window on this street. & no, you can't see the river, but look – you can tell what's given over to its brown lips

SELF-PORTRAIT WITH TRACK CHANGES

Her first in a short life
of passing from sight.

The women gather in one house.

I am a girl most when I bend
to lather feet, keen, sounding
like a drum, pulled taut and struck.

Your open door,
your tunnel.

I smooth shadow from your face
like light, thumb tears, pledge
my allegiance to allegiance.

A good daughter,
like a healthy body,
is defined by absence
of disease.

I was born on a Tuesday
with one hand in a fist. I slid
onto the earth on a cold afternoon.

When I draw you, it's in ink.

I call you some Sundays
to tell you I'm fine.

I rise in the dark to turn
the porch light back on,
most of our symptoms
briefly asleep.

NO, SUFFER HERE

from *Baker v Canada (Minister of Immigration & Citizenship)*, [1999]
2 SCR 817

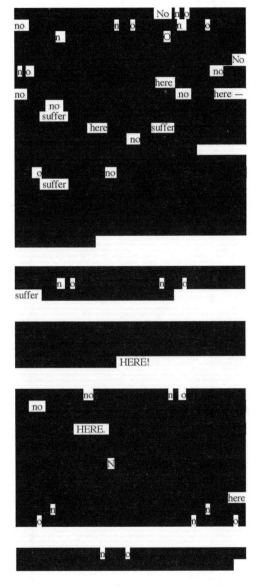

THE RHYTHM METHOD

We went to Shopper's
then for breakfast
where I tried, again,

to like eggs.
It's the texture
and the smell.

I was sure already,
the way I get sure,
obdurate and quick.

I was not sad.
We were going to go
thrifting for binoculars.

He wanted
to see the birds
but I felt a bit

nauseated, so
we went
to his place.

I watched TV.
I don't think about it, really.
I'm reaching for it here

because I am worried
that I am mostly what I want
and that I do not want

correctly, or maybe
I am worried that I do want
but can't name it

or am too afraid to name it
or that I am more
fear than desire

and I want a lot, so much.
Isn't it mechanical
if you're built like me?

Some kind of overriding
drive? I don't think
about that time

or the other times
when the answer
was as obvious

as it was hard-earned.
We would name it
August, like the poem

I can't write.
Yet another instinct
I lack.

AGAINST "MANITOBA"

Build a province of our absence,
and that province comes to pass

and it passes legislation, and the legislation
is profuse with the absence you allege.

I suggest your unseeing has its consequence.

I suggest the coasts unmoor you,
and those distant cities fit your heads.

Your bad spell echoes in this centre
of emptying centres. We measure wheat

in seeds. Your insistence follows
your gaps, a needle

leaving two holes and one stitch.

AUTO-EPITHALAMIUM

You hold up something yellow and say,
I love this yellow, and the love and the yellow

preoccupy you. This and each morning,
you rise and choose to be good, to try

to be good. Before I got home, you texted
I like you, and yes became my favourite word.

On our way anywhere, you lift a hand
for grizzled birds, for perfect blues. Near four

you cross the room, holding aloft oiled lemon
and fish, your mouth laughing questions.

Yours the back-alley lilac, toted home
to jam jar, to brown through its purpose,

to purple the air. Yours my christened shyness,
my numbered birthmarks, a long and smooth tooth.

On our second date, the day after our first,
the day before our third, you said, *This is good*,

and all four eyes were open. I want you
endless beside me, unearned, well-deserved.

I want to double light for you. This and each morning,
I am glad to be the thing under your finger,

like the pink seam where the sky never splits.

Our good life will not slip by me, slowed
under your needle, pinpointed into singing.

HEIRLOOMING

unwrap worst days unheld / scoffed a sketched lie / a
sonnet / dark on another continent / no kin to claim
/ all victor ache / lessons in verb-making make me /
a debtor / natural or normal or something obscured /
confirm by dismissing / what tints our common blood
burrows / blisters between us / unverbs / or nouns /
or ails / makes ill of us / I know in thrown bones this
unwanted centre / small stone small shoe / misthought
proximate births / misleading / belying shared moon /
reach for lifeline / grab tether / what hinders haunts us
/ what we circle / what ceaselessly centres / what you
shelve / are unable to hold / up to clearing fulgur / your
hands too full of me / your light bill / climbing

TESTIMONIUM

She shaves her head. I grow too big to hit. The neighbour bangs his broomstick against the ceiling, having forgotten all her German. Her words grow a tail for balance and speed. Something grows inside her and she almost dies. It originates somewhere and goes nowhere else. She works at a meat plant for a while. She almost marries a guy she meets in the freezer. The water calls and I answer. It snows the first time. I respond in words. She smokes cloves and sings in a choir. I learned I could bruise but had no one to tell.

ODE TO 200 FROM EACH OF MY TITS

Mostly the left one,
which is slightly smaller, less
panicked in lace, under
identical black mesh
crop top we each arrive in
having coordinated
nothing but our briefly
mirrored lives.

I mean, a red lip
and pixels do not even
approach analogy –
for one, do not convey
the body glitter
pooling.

My tits should sigh,
briefly, into gravity,
in the stall where I pull
centre-gore from chest
and swipe sweat from
under underwire.

Much like on my body,
they should feature
heavily,
revel in their first
best destiny,
high over rib cage,
belly,
ass.

You should be
crouched in the next stall,
scream-guessing lyrics
full tilt, something
juniper-sweet defying
surface tension
in a plastic shot glass.
You should be naming them
for any worthy pair: Tia and twin, Simon, Garfunkel, Hall, Oates, etc.
hallelujah, amen.

And all of us as all of us
going out, coming out, bright
under dollar-store disco ball,
over cardboard-cured potholes,
cardboard-lengthened
cocktail table legs
circled to shoulder
with every still
and unkissed girl.

My tits should be pressed
against another pair,
against the lower abdomen
of a tall person, wet
with the back sweat
of whoever will prom-pose
when demanded.
They should harden
to naming direction
when we cool onto sidewalk,
into sweet morning smoke.

They should burrow
under thrifted faux fur coat,
two live and fear-free animals.
A bosom to be spied across
a narrow, gimcrack floor,
to jiggle to VLT percussed
dancehall, to heave and heft
and be gathered into.

I should wake
hoarse from
screaming psalms
into joyful house
on joyful earth
adorned with whatever
is beautiful and nearby.
I want us together
under light scattered
by a disregarded thing
breathing identical air,
air wet with what rises
from gathered bodies,
stickied floor
a signal to stay.

LINKING RINGS
after Dean Gunnarson

You know this part well: how the pain becomes provenance. Are you afraid
something awful might happen? Several days, half the days or nearly every day?

I remember the chair and the dark, the pink skipping rope, its knots
closing in on themselves. Fear can mean reverence, which can mean feeling

small. Is your life dwindling, iris fixed on the threshold and sky? Are you
watching each mouth to guess its next shape? Did you fashion a tether

and let it tie you to your mind? A concrete image can be held like a rope.
Bound and caged over flames, there is just the cage, the mountains,

the distance, the fear and the flames. I keep achieving recognition
when I aim for the divine. There are algorithms to escape.

There's room here for self-insertion. If you build a thing to crumble,
you can be sure it will collapse. Certainty can be held like a tongue.

It can push my teeth from my head. It would leave the tender
names for those who left behind and bound me. I built a shrine

to a lifetime of untangling. From this height, it looks nothing like yours.

BYLINE CENTO

Passive voice can be recognized
from the verb phrase, which will always
include a form of be: am, is,

are, was, were, been.[1] Passive voice
reveals the writer's feelings, or
stance,[2] which does not mean

where they place their feet. Passive
voice robs subordinates of agency,
and hides the agency of dominant groups.[3]

Notice responsibility's migration[4] –
the writer's distance from the text.
If the action lacks an agent,

then that is the passive voice.
If the actor precedes the verb phrase,
then that is an active agent.

The other word for the object
the silent subject acts upon
is the patient, a word to describe

---

1 More about Passive Voice, Purdue Online Writing Lab, Purdue University. (n.d.), owl.purdue.edu/owl/general_writing/academic_writing/active_and_passive_voice/ more_about_passive_voice.html.

2 A. M. Baratta, "Revealing Stance through Passive Voice," *Journal of Pragmatics* 41, no. 8 (2009): 1406–21.

3 Nancy M. Henley et al., "Syntax, Semantics and Sexual Violence: Agency and the Passive Voice," *Journal of Language and Social Psychology* 14, nos. 1–2 (1995): 60–84.

4 T. A. Van Dijk, "Racism and Argumentation: Race Riot Rhetoric in Tabloid Editorials," *Argumentation Illuminated* (1992), 242 at 252.

someone who's fine waiting.
Passive voice acknowledges
wrongdoing without acknowledgement.[5]

Passive voice goes to suppress
referent. Interpretation
will depend, in part, on the voice

used to phrase the message[6] –
which does not say, "When the police
kills an innocent citizen ..."[7]

5 Michelle Conklin, "'Officer Involved Shootings': How the Exonerative Tense of Media Accounts Distorts Reality," *University of Miami Race & Social Justice Law Review* 12:1.

6 Nancy M. Henley et al., "Syntax, Semantics and Sexual Violence: Agency and the Passive Voice," *Journal of Language and Social Psychology* 14, nos. 1–2 (1995): 60–84.

7 T. A. Van Dijk, "Racism and Argumentation: Race Riot Rhetoric in Tabloid Editorials," *Argumentation Illuminated* (1992), 242 at 252.

SATURN APPROACHING

Still, at the doctor's, he asks me to locate the pain

and I gesture. But the upsides are a brand-new blue.

Let me tell me: I unfurl. I learn to translate

then teach. The mornings grow shorter, like a walk

feels when returning to the start. I remember

so much I won't forget — think, the strange pain of someday

driving up against my corners. It ends, though I feel it

in the key change of some songs. Can you hear me?

I think of us and weep, my face wet and unquestioned.

I wish I was here, as they say, and so the map reads:

so much of it is closing the distance the rupture grew,

my brain and hands and hollows threading themselves whole.

So much of it is naming what I was raised to call the sky.

Pick a name besides survival, like *chrysanthemum*

or *apostle* or *Blythe*. I can show my soft belly

and say anything. I will learn how to scream.

What will spark outside me was still in my inches,

grinding. Yes, I'm coming and I promise,

here I am. There is space where I echo,

and I find it, and I fill it like the fog. It works,

all the reaching, all the thirst, the blue.

I grow, like fruit does: slow and toward

sweetness, softening until we rot.

ASSEMBLAGE
after Ekene Emeka-Maduka's Morning Assembly, *2020. Oil on canvas.*

This frame is a door and the door
is closed to you. You're misreading.

Meanwhile, I make twelve cameos
in any of our pictured dozen.

Aspirants to gibberish, to dress yellows,
to unsupervised limbs, brown as good wood,

to eyes peerless and glazed, aloof
as a stone. Even now, as you watch,

or listen, or tilt thinking, tap pencil
to thinned lip, look — there I am.

Inside it: me, and me again, there too.
You, outside, misreading the text

of our face, bare as a burden. Our pause
without capture, illegible, no documentary

explaining what is clear to who is meant
to see through it. Here, emptied of your fear

well-wielded, unyielding, your questions
on our stillness. The sole threat of this assembly

is that it extends unending into an everywhere
to which you are not invited. Aspiration as in breath,

so, still, I mean breathing. The sure
unbroken math of us, the flood of us

here and coming, gang gang, tautological,
a better metaphor, your meaning empty as a throat.

Our dozens Black alive, indifferent,
half-asleep and sleeping, out of frame,

beyond it, and watching, watching back.

EPITHALAMIUM ENDING IN DEATH

I have been worrying
my bottom lip since Ms. Chang showed us

An Inconvenient Truth in Grade 10 bio,
and that's before she got sick, before Beth

told me she didn't believe in global warming,
which is what we called it then. I didn't know

you were allowed to not believe in things,
which was part of the problem

but not the whole thing. I tend to believe
very much, with my whole body.

I am trying to be romantic but I keep
thinking about the end. I read *Weather*

and *The Parable of the Sower* in one hot month
and I worried about making lamps from oil-packed tuna

mostly so I could look at you. We drove
to St. James to buy our marriage licence

from a certified issuer's suburban garage,
black bin bag backdrop lending little pomp,

and I mostly remember our listing
names and ancestors and birthplaces,

our impossible survival of the space
before each other and this

instead of the sun, smoked orange,
a doomed reminder to mark time.

I think that's nice. Every great love poem ends
in death by definition, even if implied,

and I do not lean optimistic. The best I can do
is pledge to you the balance

of my brief forever, vanishingly bright.
You can have me 'til the worms do,

and I hope the worms survive.

SPRING, OR SPIRAL IN THREE PARTS

I.

Born of dark shoulder, of bone-jut
of sinew, born of spell stretch, of touch,

its lacking. Thin gold gleams or glances.
Glance's first sense is slipperiness, now

narrows time and eyes. Look,
our distant siblings' stark departure,

look: obscuring, smoke-bright.
Time sets our mouths in a line, echoes

itself, shifts feet to steadying,
bends knees (unbuckled), bruises.

Thought the map the mountain. Oops.
I thought of a song but the song

was a border, and the border was the end.
Atlas unburdened, but then there's time

and skin and what happened
when we (us, primed and when primed,
preserved, or carved to stiff exception)

rose from genuflection, emerged
a whole and human image. What else

will we cleave? The light before
and after, the smokeless air.

Eyes arch a question,
fists clasped to fight,

not fighting.

II.

Among the best uses for my body:
bearing only numbers, counting

countless stairs to our distant
destination: the small hot room

empty of everything but a canvas
frayed and leaning, the sand pile souveniring

gelid, passing days. Last summer,
you painted every wall but the window.

I sat in the light and asked questions.
Just yesterday, yellow even from the street,

keen as a field of sunflowers,
leaning broad and beaded heads.

Maybe I'll remember these days
not for what they were, but for you

or, better, what they gave me:
places to go and a meaning,

questions and friends and new poems
revisiting remembrances,

suggesting distal points into metaphor,
the stars collapsed into constellations,

us, something less than I am.

III.

Grow new spring all wire
pause to age the quiet
to maintain force
between what otherwise
would chafe.

The universe in words:
good question.

Try small opening, brief and bested vowel.
Try spark in doomed alloy, new bounce
as slink descends steps.

There are worlds not the world
that pass like time
in corridor body.
All halls, I mean, without comment
I mean, alongside shadow
I mean space, to navigate
worthy vessel, still upright.

Destined to something sea-like but not the sea
with its borders and needs I mean
like a room reached moving through another room
or the sky, the ocean of one name.

Grow new spring, fine machine.
Cartograph, seismic scan, cord
descending spring. Ask what precedes equinox
sets precedent, sends wished-for
water subterre. In ink, I am only
my blackest parts. In own tone,
I would disappear/belong.

The lens inverts me,
hangs by wide ankle
like flank in shop window
finger-smudged. Let blood rush
and breath the body.

There are worlds that pass
like a stranger on the street,
and spin like a b-girl over half-box,
and end like the best part
of this song.

Hollow helix, turning on myself
terse ricochet, inclined to borderlessness.
What comes comes unceasing.
You learn to watch it coming,
eyes bright with what isn't the evening.

IN DEFENCE OF THE WINNIPEG POEM

It is bigger than its targets,

& still small, & there is nothing to do

& so much to be done, & here

at the centre of a bad invention,

it is, in fact, pretty cold.

SPACECRAFT

Six lights passed over us
that evening. I didn't see them. Too low,
you said, to be a plane.

You were newly alive when I met you.
You cast a blue shadow. You left
a long message, stumbling
over my names. It's true
my stomach spoke.

Did you ventriloquize me, or that evening?
One voice sang in my acquired tongue,
and the other sprouted thorns.

One face in the sun is worth
two under moon. I made my hand a visor
and you put yours around my throat:
your father's car and his cologne.

I am telling this backwards. Here, in the future,
we both have ideas. A sound emerged from me.
It was mine. I tell your story better
but I can't do it without lying.

A HISTORY OF HOUSES BUILT OUT OF SPITE

none of us know Amy personally, but she's here & she's singing / rising above our sodden heads bowed in something like prayer / maybe // most of us are trying to move enough to pretend she doesn't remind us of our mothers & Sunday morning spring cleans / the sharp bleached smell of it, the shrill peak of their voices demanding something far less beautiful // we're trying not / to think of mothers who mostly whisper now // or girls who looked away & uninvited us from sleepovers // even though they were smiling the whole time, or the last time that we were here / how it felt the same when we got home after // it as in everything // the same as in worse / you gotta move sometimes / when you're stuck in the middle of it, that's the philosophy we're buying into here / using drink tickets we bought at the dollar store & / tucked into bras & ace bandages & sagging back pockets // you gotta move // your body a last resort / occupying unceded space // the only thing that's ever belonged to you & half the girls here have called that into question // girls only because that's how you get in here / in here just because of the girls / because here is nowhere & here lives the only god that thinks our wetness akin to holy water / that answers / to the tense-bodied hallelujahs escaping mouths we thought / had forgotten how to form them // us broken daughters & all our pieces jangling // all strobe light, sweat & saxophone // when Amy died / we danced off the sorrow we knew / our mothers would shed / split their self-satisfied smugness // between us like a quarter // we tucked a backbeat under / a promise of an always love / used those tickets to buy into that sacred oath in mezzo-soprano // & we moved to it right into it // 'cause that's what the fuck you do // our love been a losing game, Amy // we know the power of no / no // no // even when it was the wrong thing / & we know we belong here / maybe not everywhere / but that's what nowhere is for / & here we are / in the middle of it // besides / it's different for us / us as in everyone // different as in   the same.

WINNIPEG POEM ("PATHETIC FALLACY")

I would tell you now I was depressed
then but then it did not need another name.
The sidewalk turned velvet with salt. I took baths
and stared, ate over the sink, shifting on and off
each ankle, convincing myself of July.
It was not special but it endured. Me too. I tended
to despair until it yellowed, overwatered.
Days launched and landed in the dark
like a film, the screen a sudden mirror
and me, surprised by the effort in my face.

COMPREHENSIVE RANKING SYSTEM

in this country of noise   I learn to speak fast

we turn to wist & salt   & gain points because

the salt is white   I am bright

but less than fluent in   questioning borders in

my mother tongue   my only country

twelve hundred points   a hole dark with want

for my father's head   where language breaks

in fractions   & then

as we shrink   breaks us

GROUND UPON

from *Baker v Canada (Minister of Immigration & Citizenship)*, [1999] 2 SCR 817

C. *Procedural Fairness*

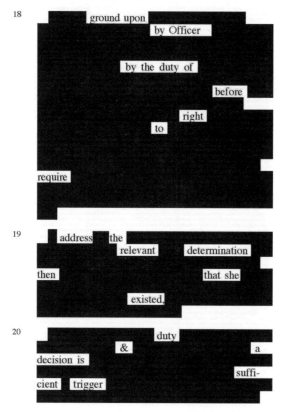

18   ground upon
by Officer

by the duty of

before

right

to

require

19   address the
relevant   determination
then   that she
existed,

20   duty
&   a
decision is
suffi-
cient   trigger

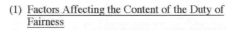

Clearly,   deter-
mination   will be
        the requirement

(1) Factors Affecting the Content of the Duty of
    Fairness

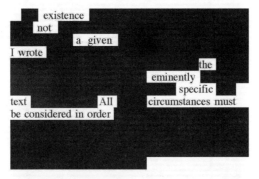

    existence
    not
            a given
I wrote
                            the
                    eminently
                        specific
text   All   circumstances must
be considered in order

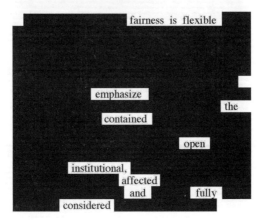

                        fairness is flexible

            emphasize
                                        the
            contained

                            open

        institutional,
            affected
                and   fully
        considered

23   Several

common

circumstances. One

is

being

held

close

the

realm of

The

body,

made to reach

making,

more likely

24   A second   nature

to

the body

the particular

protections,   will be required

when   the issue

cannot   submit

25   in determining

the impor-

tance   individual

lives

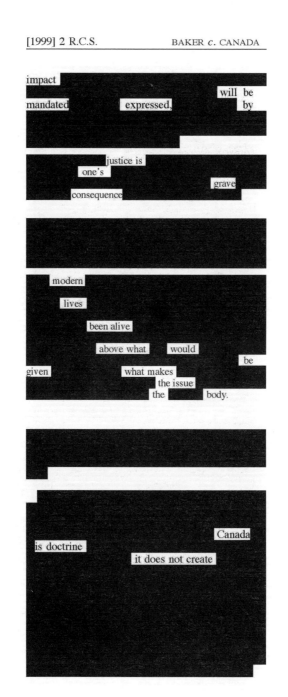

impact

will be

mandated   expressed,   by

justice is
one's
grave
consequence

modern

lives

been alive

above what   would
be
given   what makes
the issue
the   body.

Canada

is doctrine

it does not create

fairness:

or

otherwise

the doctrine of

domain.

take

act

backtrack

promise

27

the analysis of

choice of

the ability to choose

or an expertise in

circumstances:

determina-

tive,

constraints:

28

These principles
the procedures

the duty

the

opportunity

their rights, interests,

privileges   an

institutional,

decision.

PHONE HOME

There is much
              less than a country
              between us,
              depending on how you draw the country.

There is much less than an ocean.

My favourite colour
has not been blue in years.

SEARCH HISTORY
after Leila Chatti

how will	[I know lyrics]
how will	[they hear without a preacher]
how will	[the world end]
how long	[does covid last]
how long	[does it take to get a passport]
how long	[does it take to get to the moon]
how long do we	
how much	[protein per day]
how much	[caffeine in coffee]
how much	[protein in one egg]
how much	[mortgage can I afford]
how much	[is a stick of butter]
how much longer	[will the sun last]
how much longer	[till the world ends]
how much longer	[till summer]
how much time	[have I wasted on league]
how much time	[between]
how much time	[is left]
how much time	[to boil eggs]
how much time do	[we spend sleeping]
how much time do	[we have to save the planet]
how much time do	[you need for a layover]
how much time do	[we have left]
how much time do	[I have left]
how much time do	[we have left]

FIELD GUIDE TO THE BIRDS OF NORTH AMERICA
with three lines from Wikipedia

The black-capped chickadee is a small
non-migratory North American songbird that lives
in deciduous and mixed forests
and in the elm by the resource centre
whose soft rotting bark it beaked
soft or hollow enough to lay black cap
and in the wax rendering one
of the three youths in group
who named themselves for water
etched unsmiling onto dark
cardboard so the bird is mostly
shimmer and suggestion
and briefly in the window
right before it split the glass
and in the cropped gym t-shirt
Sam used to build a nest
cradled with her finger
on her best guess at its throat
and in flocks of four to twelve
in mated pairs and if young
unmoored from other populations
and on fences and wires
every horizontal edge the city hesitates
and they die in such numbers
with such specificity that scientists
name it and watch unmoved
a crooked finger at their chin
and in Ocean who went
to name themself in this room
of self-naming of calling
ourselves and learning to answer
and chose water never seen very far away
and in the mural for their sibling

whose fosters won't let come to group
and in the YouTube video
because this bird has lived drowned out
by helicopter call and siren song
and bless Sam's heart is probably dead
but the kids still want to know
what sound it would have made

CONFIGURATION

Black commas syncopating sky,
corvids perched on midnight wire.
Neither omen nor a knife
black and black-beaked and indifferent.

Corvids perched on midnight wire,
fat with analysis and circumstance,
black and black-beaked and indifferent,
haunting Young & Portage.

Fat with analysis and circumstance,
and clean of all insistent meaning,
haunting Young & Portage,
where tied kicks swing inky.

Clean of all insistent meaning,
many nights are only nights
where tied kicks swing inky,
mark some other nothing.

Many nights are only nights
miscalled in terms of venery.
Mark some other nothing
with its dark implications.

Miscalled in terms of venery,
haunting is wrong, like *dark* is
with its dark implications.
It's just there they are.

Haunting is wrong, like *dark* is.
Black commas syncopating sky.
It's just there they are,
never an omen, not a knife.

SENTENCING FACTORS

All circumstances must be considered in order —
chronological, if time is your god, which it will be
if you're not god. If you are, I have questions for you:

like when in the story did you arrive? If you were god,
you'd know the right answer is after all the suffering began.
We can all agree that providence is a fucked fluxus game,

an odd way to determine the importance of individual lives,
just like we can all agree that a margin is an edge. And that's just
what I would start to say if you asked me,

which you would if you weren't god. The gaps are easier
to see if you know and love well the thrown-through

who green text and call collect and climb
their slow way toward you, you not-gods perched
on the platform of mistakes that other people never made

and made, mistakes that would never
have occurred to you, other things being possible,
possibility being the other thing.

FACT PATTERN

from *Smithers v the Queen*, [1978] 1 SCR 506

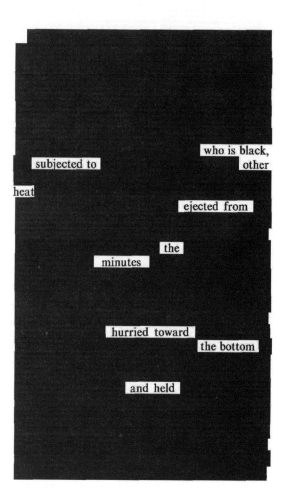

TATTLETALE

I was literate in air. I was small and extrasensory. I grew a weather vane I can't describe. I watched rage bequeath itself and felt it and fled it, am fleeing. How do you say I sat at its table, both hands cupping my jaw. Foreshadow's mnemonic: the swing of the door, your hand on the still-warm TV. I thought we were just like this. I thought I would be. I rode the arc of your span. I learned the value of distance, the futility of teeth. Baby missteps earned cruelty and sibilant air and appellations I call myself and can't, having received mostly aftershock and hand-me-downs. I was very small and a good inventor. Even now, slanting through, I'm all spackle, all language, and absent even that, weeping what I cannot say.

I COULD SHRINK WHAT SHRUNK ME

"I never was a child — soon as I popped out of my mom, I was just in the know."
—Tiffany "New York" Pollard

I could shrink what shrunk me,
ramble through dusk in the same blue
the day would. I could sound out
my cue cards, arrive with price tags

on my clothes, make my breadth
a tribute posing as a premonition,
reminding me of my own name,
which is a guess that someone took.

I could wax tragic and convincing,
each mood rising to the surface
like a swimmer taking breath.
I could remain available to myself.

I could yield to the right knife's
right angle, curl my tin like a can
of fish: the rows of scales,
the eyes that almost see.

ERRATUM
after Nikki Wallschlaeger

against novel misnomer – against *et cetera*, erratum, apologia – against tumid oratory – against going sans attending – against echo's prescience – against unaccounting, fractured calculus – against government god – against our briefly hoisted faces, their Vaseline and sweat glisten – against unmuffled murmur – against *body* meaning me – against *listening and learning and trying to do better* – against centring, circling centre – against normal – against ordinarying – (again: rebellion from bellum (from bellyache, surely)) – against certainty – against sickle – against blackened quire – against expendability – (again: whole begets holy) – (again: plait fingers (form duke)) – against fist, or flesh, or language – against logging in ledger – against countability – against sheet or fine fescue – riverbound in dress yellow – against pale palms, dark fingers – against skin, shifting on time's broad throat

AN INFORMED PERSON

from *Baker v Canada (Minister of Immigration & Citizenship)*, [1999] 2 SCR 817

(5) <u>Reasonable Apprehension of Bias</u>

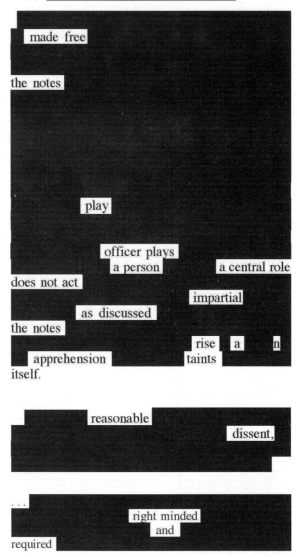

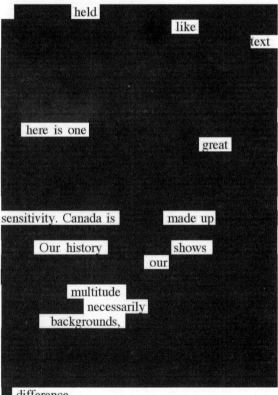

viewing

the matter

unconsciously,

held

like

text

here is one

great

sensitivity. Canada is   made up

Our history   shows

our

multitude

necessarily

backgrounds,

difference.

WINNIPEG POEM ("PORTAGE")

Burden
from need.
Do and then don't
and without
would have
swallowed
the river.
I survived
and feel survival
in my arms
what's brought
over water
and then hung
over head.

QUIET DOG
after Nicole Sealey

Mos Def, I owe you an apology —

My recall won't let you define
yourself, resists redefinition.

Nostalgia is undefeated,
determined to mistake reform for deform,

insists you remain fantasy: definite,
deific and utmost. I'll defend

the first half (half-heartedly), when you defused
my fear of mankind, warm eyes of indefinite

depth a tender promise. It's my deficient
follow-up at fault. I dreamed you definitional,

the man after which other men are defenestrated,
demarcating perfection by ignoring defect.

Not that I know you — better to defer
to stans and historians than my prideful

misponderings, romantic with defence.
I was sure from pictures you'd deflower

me (after marriage), your attentions fluent and deft
as this poem, which tucks in *def* from Mos Def,

a name for you that you now defy,
like I defy any truth that would defoliate

and unspring the very sprung. The truth defaces
the carefully rendered, defrocks

holy fantasy. Which — yeah, is definitely
in this case, my bad. I un/made you (indefensible),

grew mad at your hands. My mind, indefatigable.
I guess I just want what's undefiled

by whatever's real. A quiet dog, defanged.

SORRY CENTO

An apology is an expression
of sympathy or regret.[1] In some nations,

an acknowledgment will suffice. An apology
is not necessarily an admission of guilt.

In some places, an apology means something
like not sorry. A good apology can be

a humiliating act. A good apology may detract
from the apologizer's symbolic power.[2]

An apology is remedial work,
a gesture which splits the individual

into two parts.[3] An acknowledgement
of responsibility may express self-deficiency.[4]

An apology should include an explanation or account.
An explicit expression might be an offer of apology.

For example, I am sorry. An explicit expression
might be a request for forgiveness. An acknowledgment

of responsibility may offer
repair or redress. For example,

---

1 *The Apology Act*, ccsm c A98.

2 Z. Kampf, "Public (non-)apologies: The Discourse of Minimizing Responsibility," *Journal of Pragmatics* 41, no. 11 (2009): 2257–70.

3 E. Goffman, "Remedial work," in *Life as Theater: A Dramaturgical Sourcebook*, ed. Dennis Brissett and Charles Edgley, 2nd ed. (Pascatiway, NJ: Transaction Publishers, 2005).

4 J. Holmes, "Apologies in New Zealand English," *Language in Society* 19, no. 2 (1990): 155–99.

I will make it up to you.
An apology is an illocutionary force,

wherein the truth of the expressed proposition
is pre-supposed.[5] The defining features of an apology

are admissions of blameworthiness
and regret for an undesirable event.[6]

An acknowledgement of responsibility
is part of a good apology. For example,

accepting the blame. A good apology
includes a promise of forbearance.

For example, it will never happen again.

---

5 J. R. Searle, "A Taxonomy of Illocutionary Acts," in *Expression and Meaning: Studies in the Theory of Speech Acts* (Cambridge: Cambridge University Press, 1979).

6 B. R. Schlenker and B. W. Darby, "The Use of Apologies in Social Predicaments." *Social Psychology Quarterly* 44, no. 3 (1981): 271–78.

CALL IN

This can't be the work my freedom needs. The nannying?
The audience behind his waiting, cocksure head? Forgive me,
but there would be committees. The emails would be awful —
so long — and anyway, where would this apology go?
My ledger is painstaked, overlined in blue ink. Is this
on me? I can't concern myself with everything I'm owed.
I wouldn't have enough time to go out some Saturdays.
And how would I explain why I started to laugh? Like this:
it was his ease. It was what it evoked, all of which
would be denied: his closed car windows, his eight fingers rapped
on post-racial steering wheel. Too, the telling, a reprise,
told first, I'd bet, to swallows but with colour in each cheek.
Then, that ending A, soft and open, an empty space,
his mouth still smiling around it, braced for a modern song.

NOTES

"Escapology" and "Linking Rings": Dean Gunnarson is a Canadian escapologist.

"360 Portage": The poem's title is the address of the Manitoba Hydro building in downtown Winnipeg. The lines "a clean, green engineering marvel" and "a growing hunger for power in the South is fed" are paraphrased from APTN's *Power—Christopher Read*, a documentary about the impact of hydroelectric dams on Indigenous communities in Manitoba.

The erasures of Supreme Court of Canada cases owe an intellectual debt to Dr. Amar Khoday's "Black Voices Matter Too: Counter Narrating Smithers v The Queen," *Osgoode Hall Law Journal* 58.3 (2021) : 567–621.

"Song for Endling, Unborn": The poem's title is after Diane di Prima's "Song for Baby-O, Unborn."

"Quiet Dog": This poem is inspired by Nicole Sealey's "An Apology for Trashing Magazines in Which You Appear." The poem's title is after "Quiet Dog Bite Hard" by Yasiin Bey (formerly known as Mos Def).

"Spring, or Spiral in Three Parts": This poem was originally commissioned by Patterns Collective and Gallery 1C03 for *Sanctuaries: A Virtual Exhibition*, which featured work by Anique Jordan, Akum Maduka, and Rajni Perera.

"Search History": This conceit poem is after Leila Chatti's poem "Google."

"A History of Houses Built Out of Spite": The poem's title is after "A Brief History of Houses Built Out of Spite." the *Bloomberg* article by John Metcalfe.

Thank you to all the editors who published previous versions of these poems:

- "Grunthal, Manitoba (2019)" appeared in *Poetry Is Dead*.

- "On the Imminent Destruction of Portage Place Mall" appeared in *Canadian Literature*.

- "Girls Who" appeared in *CV2 Magazine*.

- "Auto-Epithalamium" and "Epithalamium Ending in Death" appeared in *Canthius*.

- "Erratum" appeared in *Brick*.

- "A History of Houses Built Out of Spite" was published by Akashic Books in my chapbook, *The Habitual Be*, which was included in *New-Generation African Poets: A Chapbook Box Set (Nne)*.

ACKNOWLEDGEMENTS

Here's my language at its limits: how to thank all of you, and to thank you all enough. I owe more gratitude than I can fit here, but here is a start:

My family, gifted, lucked into and chosen.

My friends, whom I love very deeply and mostly decline to list. For walking me towards Sci/Mar, shoutout to Schmozby, true blue, for the headshot and our whole life, Chukwudubem, for the books, links, and walks, Victo, for the phone calls and the earrings, and Sab, the other poet in my head.

Kevin Connolly, LJ Ahenda, Stuart Ross, and the whole team at Anansi, your hope and guidance, your attention, and commas, and care.

Canisia, Katherena, and Sanna, for seeing these poems so clearly and saying so kindly what it is you see. You three, again, and all the other poets and writers I admire, who make and remake me.

The rest of the ruckus: jaye, Lou, Cooper, Nicole, Aaron, for the noise and its echoes. The Emotional Historians, on Mondays by lamplight.

The Winnipeg arts community, the best thing about a good place. QPOC Winnipeg, for holding all of me, at the protests, the parties, the performances.

All my teachers and mentors in language, linguistics, law and life, for rewarding and directing curiosity and courage for the last thirty years.

Dear reader, for allowing these poems into your lives.

Nathan, my love, who built me a writing desk from an old piano, who makes me laugh every day. God only knows what I'd be without you.

© Imalka Nilmalgoda

CHIMWEMWE UNDI is a poet, editor, and lawyer living and writing on Treaty 1 territory in Winnipeg, Manitoba. Her work has appeared in *Brick*, *Border Crossings*, *Canadian Literature*, and BBC World, among others. She was the recipient of the 2022 John Hirsch Emerging Writer Award from the Manitoba Book Awards, and she is the Winnipeg Poet Laureate for 2023 and 2024.